Sorry Abou

A Lean Guide to Reducing Wait Times

and Improve Customer Experience

Eduardo J. Estrada

Sorry About the Wait

Eduardo J. Estrada

Published by Eduardo J. Estrada, 2023.

SORRY ABOUT THE WAIT

First edition. April 24, 2023.

Copyright © 2023 Eduardo J. Estrada.

ISBN: 979-8215933152

Written by Eduardo J. Estrada.

Table of Contents

This Book is dedicated to my Family, Parents and All Frontline workers that serve so many other fellow Humans.

Introduction

HAVE YOU EVER FOUND yourself in a retail or hospitality business, patiently waiting for your order to arrive, only to be met with an apologetic "sorry about the wait" from the service staff? If so, you're not alone. This common issue inspired the creation of this book - a guide that explores the tested Lean Manufacturing ideas applied to the hospitality industry and small businesses.

You've probably picked up this book and wondered, I heard a similar phrase many times, but how exactly is this book going to help me?

The problem this book is trying to resolve, and help you with, is to find a way to accelerate the time from order to service delivery, while increasing your customer's experience.

As an experienced industrial engineer who has helped businesses to improve their operations, I aim to condense and explore some of the already tested Lean Manufacturing concepts and relate them to the hospitality industry and small business processes, while also enhancing customer experience.

The book's approach is simple and practical, encouraging you to start with the basics and build your way up to mastery. Each tool and technique are explained in detail, with examples of how you apply them in a real-world setting.

As with any skill it is important to test, learn, apply your learnings and keep continually improving.

Regardless of your definition of success, whether it be financial gain or simply providing the best possible experience for your customers, this book is designed to help you achieve your goals. It's a guide that can be used as a starting point, a reference, and a source of inspiration for anyone who wants to improve their business operations and deliver the best possible experience to their customers.

So, if you're ready to take the first step towards improving your business, start by reading this book; put the tools and techniques into practice and see how they can help you achieve your goals. Share your journey and your successes with your team, and together, you can create a culture of continuous improvement that will benefit your business and your customers alike.

It will be great to hear about your journey, your learnings and even better your improved customer reviews.

PART I: Building Blocks for a Great Experience

DELIVERING GREAT CUSTOMER experiences is more important than ever in today's highly competitive business landscape. Businesses across all industries are heavily investing in customer experience programs to attract and retain customers, from retail stores and restaurants to hospitals and airlines.

But what does it take to provide a memorable customer experience? What are the building blocks that businesses must focus on to provide memorable experiences that keep your customers returning?

As an industrial engineer working with businesses to improve their operations, I've discovered there are several critical building blocks to creating a great customer experience. Understanding customer needs and expectations, as well as optimising processes, are examples of these building blocks. In this chapter, we will explore the customer experience and operations improvements building blocks in more detail to incorporate them into business.

Whether you are a business owner, a hospitality service provider or a customer experience manager looking to improve your operations, this part will provide you with a brief and valuable insight of customer experience and lean management.

Chapter 1: Understanding Customer Experience

"Your most unhappy customers are your greatest source of learning." – Bill Gates

WHEN WAS THE LAST TIME that you've heard someone say, "Sorry About the Wait"? Was it in a café, restaurant, pharmacy or maybe in a service business? Regardless of the context, these words imply the customer's experience was not up to your expectations.

Nowadays, we expect a faster service and a more pleasant atmosphere, but sometimes things go wrong, and we leave a retail or business place dissatisfied.

According to recent research (Waitwhile, 2022) "Nearly 69% of those surveyed said that waiting in line elicits negative feelings, including boredom, annoyance, frustration, and impatience. Remarkably, fewer than 3% of respondents associated waiting with something positive to look forward to ("Excited")".

In this chapter, we will discuss ways to measure excellent customer experience in Lean Manufacturing and how quality management systems put emphasis on customer surveys and satisfaction to improve customer experience.

Customer Experience (CX) is a critical aspect of any business, and it can make or break a company's success. CX refers to the overall experience that a customer has when interacting with a brand, including their interactions with employees, the products or services offered, and the overall atmosphere and service of the business.

What is Customer Experience and Why is it Important?

I WOULD SUMMARISE CUSTOMER experience as the sum of all touchpoints from finding about the business into all the journey of the customer interactions including the business post-purchase follow-ups.

If any of those touchpoints fall into the cracks, the customer experience can suffer and the customer would consciously or unconscientiously decide if they would continue the relationship with the business.

A customer experience can also include touchpoints such as advertising, website, social media, customer service, sales, and after-sales support. Customer experience is critical because it can make or break a customer's loyalty to a business.

Positive customer experience can lead to repeat business, increased customer satisfaction, and positive word-of-mouth marketing, while negative customer experience can lead to loss of customers and negative reviews.

As I was researching for this book, I found a survey conducted by PwC (PwC, 2018), where they mention that "73% of consumers identified customer experience as an important factor in their purchasing decisions. And nearly 80% of surveyed consumers point to speed, convenience, knowledgeable help, and friendly service as the most important elements of a positive customer experience."

These statistics highlight the growing importance of customer experience in any industry, and the impact that it can have on a company's success.

At the end companies that excel at customer experience grow revenue faster than their competitors who do not.

With the increasing use of technology and the changing expectations of customers, it's becoming more critical than ever for organizations to focus on delivering an excellent customer experience to stay competitive in the market.

In a survey conducted by Zendesk (ZenDesk, 2022), "64% of surveyed under 40 report that customer service feels like an afterthought for most of the businesses they buy from."

Customer experience has become an essential component of business success because it directly impacts customer satisfaction and loyalty. Satisfied customers are more likely to become repeat customers and recommend the business to others, while dissatisfied customers are likely to take their business elsewhere and share their negative experience with others.

Moreover, customer experience is closely tied to a company's brand reputation. A company with a reputation for providing excellent customer experience is more likely to attract new customers and retain existing ones, leading to increased sales and revenue.

Challenges in Delivering Excellent Customer Experience

NOWADAYS WITH SOME claiming that our attention spans are getting shorten the challenges of keeping a customer engaged are decreasing either online or in the physical world.

Experts like Nick Morgan (PhD, 2021) say that, "Online, attention spans do seem to have become shorter—seven to 10 minutes seems about right".

In your service or business, understanding customer experience is critical to providing an exceptional experience to customers. Also, since 2021 and part of the residual effects of the pandemic, the average wait times for getting a service have been also affected by labour shortages, parts shortages and other supply chain issues. There are even more blogs appearing about how to say sorry to customers as seems to be "the most effective, cheapest way to turn around a bad customer experience" according to Sarah Chambers (Chambers, n.d.)Many organizations struggle to deliver excellent customer experience and seems that the common challenges that businesses face on this regard are:

- Siloed Departments: Lack of communication and collaboration among different departments which lead to inconsistencies in customer experience.
- Employee Engagement: Unengaged employees who are not empowered to make decisions can negatively impact customer experience. This includes heavy workloads or the amount of work on their plate.
- Inefficient Processes: Inefficient processes can lead to long wait times and frustration for customers.
- Inadequate Training: Inadequate training of employees can lead to a lack of knowledge and skills to deliver excellent customer experience.
- Understanding customer expectations: Customers have unique expectations for their experience with a brand, and it's important for organizations to understand and meet these expectations. However, with a diverse customer base, understanding these expectations can be challenging.
- Providing consistent service: Providing consistent service across all locations and employees can be challenging, particularly in large organizations.
- Managing customer complaints: Dealing with customer complaints can be stressful, and not all employees have the necessary skills or training to handle them effectively.
- Integrating technology: While technology can improve customer experience, integrating it into the customer

experience can be challenging and requires careful planning and execution.

Later, I'm going to explain some tools and techniques associated to Lean Methods that you can use to improve your customer's experience.

Ways to measure Excellent Customer Experience

WITH CUSTOMER EXPERIENCE becoming so critical nowadays, you'll need a way to measure it so can continuously improve it.

In today's competitive business environment, delivering excellent customer experience has become critical for the success and growth of any organization. Customer experience is the sum of all interactions that a customer has with a company, from the first contact to the after-sales service.

In Lean Manufacturing, customer experience is an essential aspect of quality management, which aims to provide products and services that meet or exceed customer expectations.

Even the quality management systems put emphasis in customer surveys and satisfaction as this can tell your business ways to improve the interactions with your customers.

Measuring customer experience involves collecting and analysing data on customer interactions with a company. There are several ways to measure customer experience, including:

Customer Surveys: Customer surveys are an effective way to collect feedback from customers about their experience with a company. Surveys can be conducted through various channels such as email, phone, or online. They can include questions about the customer's satisfaction with the product or service, the ease of doing business with the company, and the overall experience. The data collected from customer surveys can be used to identify areas of improvement and to develop strategies to enhance customer experience.

Net Promoter Score (NPS): NPS is a widely used metric to measure customer loyalty and satisfaction. It is calculated by asking customers a simple question: "On a scale of 0-10, how likely are you to recommend our product/service to others?" Based on their response, customers are classified as promoters (9-10), passives (7-8), or detractors (0-6). The NPS score is calculated by subtracting the percentage of detractors from the percentage of promoters. NPS provides businesses with valuable insights into customer satisfaction and loyalty and helps them identify areas for improvement.

Customer Effort Score (CES): CES measures how easy it is for customers to interact with a business and get their problem solved. It is calculated by asking customers a simple question: "How easy was it to get your problem solved?" Based on their response, customers are classified as having a low effort (1-3), medium effort (4-6), or high effort (7-10) experience. The lower the CES score, the better the customer experience.

Mystery shoppers: Another example of continuous improvement in retail and hospitality is the use of mystery shoppers. Mystery shoppers are individuals who are hired to visit businesses and provide feedback on their experiences. By collecting this feedback, businesses can identify areas for improvement and make changes to processes and systems that will lead to better customer experiences.

Chapter Summary/Key Takeaways

- Customer experience is a critical aspect of any business, and critical for any face-to-face businesses like in hospitality.
- Customer experience directly impacts customer satisfaction, loyalty, and brand reputation.
- Tools and techniques such as surveys can be used constantly in your business to improve the customer experience.
- By focusing on customer experience and continually improving it, your organization can attract new customers, retain existing ones, and ultimately, drive business success.

EDUARDO J. ESTRADA

Chapter 2: Introduction to Lean Manufacturing

"There is nothing so useless as doing efficiently that which should not be done at all." – Peter F. Drucker

CONSIDERING THAT THERE are so many incredibly good books and guides about lean manufacturing, this would a simple introduction so you can see why Lean becomes relevant for a great customer experience.

With the original purpose of increasing productivity and efficiency in the manufacturing industry, a new set of tools known as Lean Manufacturing were created.

To enhance the customer experience, these concepts can also be used in other sectors like retail and hospitality. The main ideas of Lean Manufacturing will be shown in this chapter, along with examples of how they can be used in the retail and hospitality sectors to cut waste and enhance the consumer experience.

Lean Philosophy

LEAN MANUFACTURING Philosophy started as a way to give only added-value to the customers, hence anything that is not value added is not helping the purpose.

According to the lean philosophy, "Value" is any action or process that the customer pays for or is willing to pay for.

Some other key principles of Lean Manufacturing, include the continuous improvement, waste reduction, value stream mapping and visual management, which can be easily applied to the retail and hospitality industries to reduce waste and improve customer experience.

The history of the Lean Manufacturing philosophy can be traced back to the industrial revolution with Fredrick Taylor and Henry Ford's manufacturing techniques to optimise resources.

Another great contributor to the Lean and Quality Management tools was Dr. Edwards Deming who has been credited with initiating Total Quality Management (TQM) and helped Toyota Motor Company, Motorola, and others to implement his TQM methods and develop Lean procedures and tools.

Many companies discovered a strong link between greater productivity and better quality during the development of Lean and Quality management, implying that having best-in-class quality does not necessitate additional effort; in fact, companies with the greatest productivity were also the best in quality.

Nowadays the Toyota Production Method as it is known or, TPM as its acronym, of Lean approaches around the world, which focuses on waste elimination and process continuous improvements.

While the TPM was getting developed, they started one of the big principles of Lean which is Just in Time that can be defined as doing nothing until the customer requires you to do something. Doing something usually should start with a in the form of an order, when basically the clock starts ticking to deliver.

One of the most suitable definitions of Lean for the objectives of this book is by Mr. John Shook, who said that "Lean is a philosophy which shortens the time between the customer order and the product build/ shipment by eliminating sources of waste."

Waste

MAYBE NOW IS A GOOD time to introduce the concept of Waste in Lean, which is a bit different to the normal definition of trash or garbage.

According to the Lean philosophy, Waste can be defined as any activity or process that does not add value to the customer. Examples include material, time and resources that are not getting used to add value.

In retail and hospitality, waste can take many forms, including overproduction, excess inventory, waiting, unused talents and defects.

By reducing waste, businesses can improve efficiency and reduce costs, which can lead to improved customer experiences.

In Chapter 3, we would expand about some other examples and standard definitions of Waste which should spark some improvement ideas for your business.

Continuous Improvement

CONTINUOUS IMPROVEMENT is another core principle of Lean Manufacturing. It is the process of making incremental improvements to processes, systems, and products to increase efficiency and effectiveness.

This can also be defined as the principle of "aggregate marginal gains" and is the idea that if you improve by just 1% consistently, those small gains will add up to significant improvements in the long term.

This principle is also normally referred in the Lean philosophy with a Japanese term called Kaizen, which is normally considered a synonym of continuous improvement.

Kaizen can be used to improve the quality of products and services by continuously making small changes to processes and systems. For example, in a hospitality business, Kaizen can be used to identify and eliminate waste, reduce costs, and enhance the customer experience.

In retail and hospitality, continuous improvement can be achieved by implementing processes that encourage feedback from customers and employees. By collecting feedback, businesses can identify areas for improvement and make changes to processes and systems that will lead to better customer experiences.

Collecting and acting on appropriate feedback is a great way of continuously improving customer experience while refining your business culture.

Several tools can be used to achieve continuous improvement in customer experience. One of the most common is the Voice of the Customer (VOC) program. This program collects feedback from customers to identify their needs, expectations, and preferences. This information is then used to improve the organization's products, services, and processes.

Chapter Summary/Key Takeaways

- The key principles of Lean Manufacturing are focused in increasing customer value, while improving efficiency in business.
- Waste reduction is one of the principles that lead to elimination of costs and non-value-added process.
- Continuous improvement can be applied to any process to reduce waste and improve customer experience.
- By implementing these principles, businesses can improve efficiency, reduce costs, and create a better overall customer experience.

PART II: Tools At Hand

WHEN PROBLEMS SEEM so big it can get overwhelming, especially when not having the right experience or tool to solve it.

Fortunately, there are several tools and techniques that you can use to improve your customer experience.

The second part of this book is to show some Lean tools that have been tried and tested for decades, which should give you great results. Not all tools are listed here because there are great resources available out there, so you can keep adding to your knowledge and improvements. The purpose of this part is to show some of the practical tools available from Lean that you can use in your business environment.

Chapter 3: Basic Tools

———

"I suppose it is tempting, if the only tool you have is a hammer, to treat everything as if it were a nail." – Abraham Maslow

SOMETIMES WHEN WE HEAR basic tools, it can mean just having the minimum needed to achieve all possible jobs.

We have learned from experiences that the extremes are not always good, either too little or too complex, which can also relate to the use of tools to solve problems in your business.

In the society that we live, sometimes simple is better and this is what I want to highlight here, the simple basic tools that will give you the better outcome for the time spent improving.

The idea of having some of the basic tools in your operation is that you can build on top of that and start using more advanced tools later. This chapter gives a basic overview of Lean tools that can be used to reduce waste and improve operations in your business and service.

In the chapter 4, we will expand with some examples, templates and cases to use these tools.

If you keep in mind that the objective of the problem-solving tools is to identify and eliminate waste in your operations while improving your customer experience, then you will find great value in using them frequently.

Kaizen or Continuous Improvement Framework

ALTHOUGH SOME KAIZEN or improvements can be analysed and implemented quickly, there are other situation where you need more time and analysing before improving.

The standard steps to implement an improvement can be based in the continuous improvement Plan-Do-Check-Act (PDCA) cycle. This cycle involves four stages: planning, executing, checking, and acting.

It is a very efficient approach to problem-solving that can enable you and your team to identify issues, develop solutions, implement them, and monitor their effectiveness.

The steps that you can use are:

Plan

1. Defining the problem or opportunity for improvement. Defining the Team.
2. Gathering data to understand the current process or system.
3. Brainstorming and analysing the current information or data.

Do

1. Developing and implementing the proposed solutions to address the identified issues.

Check

1. Evaluating the effectiveness of the solutions and adjusting as needed.

Act

1. Standardising the improved process or system either in a work instruction or visual guide, to ensure continuous improvement over time.

Lean Waste Audit and Framework

AS MENTIONED IN PART 1, waste can also be defined as anything in your operation that doesn't add value to the customer.

In today's business climate, offering excellent client experience is essential for any organisation's success. However, providing excellent customer service can be difficult, especially when waste occurs in the process.

It is critical to find and eliminate waste in any process to enhance customer experience. A tool that you can use to minimise waste in operations is a Lean Waste Audit which contains eight different kinds of wastes. This tool is normally based in the TIM WOODS framework.

The TIM WOODS framework is an acronym that has been used as part of the Waste Audit tools in lean management, to identify and eliminate waste in processes.

The acronym stands for:

- Transport
- Inventory
- Motion
- Waiting
- Overproduction
- Overprocessing
- Defects
- Skills

By identifying and eliminating waste in each of these areas, you can streamline your business processes and improve the efficiency and effectiveness of customer experience. Let's see some basic definitions.

Transport

Transport waste occurs when unnecessary movement of people or products is required. In the any process, this can include unnecessary transfers of information or equipment between departments. For example, to reduce transport waste in customer service, organizations can use tools such as value stream mapping to identify areas where transportation can be reduced or eliminated.

Inventory

Inventory waste occurs when more inventory is produced or maintained than is needed. An example for a customer service process can include excessive inventory of customer data or equipment. To reduce inventory waste, you can use tools such as just-in-time (JIT) production to produce only what is needed when it is needed.

Motion

Motion waste occurs when unnecessary movement of people or equipment is required. In the service process, this can include excessive movement to make a simple cup of coffee while serving a customer or passing customer data between departments. To reduce motion waste in your operations, you can use tools such as the Spaghetti Diagram or 6S (Sort, Set in Order, Shine, Standardize, Sustain and Safety) to improve workplace organization and reduce unnecessary movement.

Waiting

Waiting waste occurs when time is wasted waiting for a process to complete. In a process, this can include waiting for customer data or equipment to be processed. To reduce waiting waste in customer service, organizations can use tools such as Kanban to manage inventory levels and production schedules, reducing the need for customers to wait for products to be produced.

Overproduction

Overproduction waste occurs when more products or services are produced than is needed. In the customer service process, this can include producing too much food or too much data or widgets. To reduce overproduction waste, you can use tools such as flow production to produce only what is needed when it is needed.

Overprocessing

Overprocessing waste occurs when more work is done than is needed to produce a product or service. In the customer service process, this can include performing unnecessary tasks or using overly complex systems to process customer data or equipment. To reduce overprocessing waste, you can use tools such as value stream mapping to identify areas where overprocessing can be reduced or eliminated.

Defects

Defect waste occurs when errors or defects are produced in the production process. In the customer service process, this can include incorrect customer orders or incorrect service delivery. To reduce defect waste, you can use tools such as mistake-proofing to prevent errors from occurring in the first place.

Skills

Skills waste occurs when employees are not fully utilised or their skills are not being improved effectively. In your service or process, this can include underutilizing the skills of customer service representatives. To improve skills, you can use tools such as coaching, training, job rotation to cross-train employees, improving their skills and making them more versatile in their roles.

Using Value Stream Mapping to Improve Customer Experience

VALUE STREAM MAPPING is a tool that is used to identify the steps in a process that add value to the customer and those that do not. By identifying these steps, businesses can identify areas for improvement and make changes to processes that will lead to better customer experiences.

For example, in retail and hospitality businesses, value stream mapping can be used to identify the steps in the customer journey that add value and those that do not. Customer journey mapping is another similar tool that helps organizations understand the customer's journey from initial contact to post-purchase experience.

By identifying these steps, businesses can make changes to processes that will lead to better customer experiences. For example, if value stream mapping identifies that the checkout process is slow and frustrating for customers, businesses can make changes to the process to improve speed and efficiency.

By mapping out each step of the journey, organizations can identify areas where they can improve the customer experience.

The standard process to do a value stream map include:

1. **Choose a process to map:** Identify the process that you want to map and improve. It could be a specific area of your business, such as production or customer service.
2. **Assemble a team:** Select a team of individuals who are familiar with the process and have the expertise in your process. The

team could include managers, supervisors, and front-line employees.

3. **Collect data:** Gather data on the process being mapped, including cycle times, lead times, inventory levels, and other relevant metrics.

4. **Draw a current state map:** Create a visual representation of the current process, including the flow of materials and information, process steps, and any bottlenecks or waste. This is typically done using a flowchart or process map.

5. **Identify areas of waste:** Analyse the current state map to identify areas of waste, such as excess inventory, overproduction, and waiting time. Use the 8 types of waste (TIM WOODS) as a guide.

6. **Develop a future state map:** Based on the analysis of the current state map, create a visual representation of the ideal process, including changes to eliminate waste and improve flow.

7. **Implement improvements:** Use the future state map as a guide to implement improvements to the process. This may involve changes to layout, equipment, or procedures.

8. **Monitor progress:** Track the process over time to measure progress and identify further opportunities for improvement.

Spaghetti Diagram

ONE EFFECTIVE TOOL from Lean Management that can be used to reduce motion in a restaurant or service business is the "Spaghetti Diagram." A spaghetti diagram is a visual representation (like a bunch of spaghetti thrown on a piece of paper) of the movement of employees, equipment, and supplies in a workspace.

By mapping out the flow of people and materials, you can identify areas of unnecessary motion and waste, and then work to eliminate them.

To create a spaghetti diagram, start by drawing a map of their workspace, including all the equipment and workstations. Then, observe the movement of employees and materials, recording the paths they take on the map. The resulting diagram can then be analysed to identify areas where motion can be reduced.

By reducing motion, you can improve your team's productivity and efficiency, while also reducing the risk of employee injury and fatigue. This can lead to a more streamlined and effective work environment, ultimately improving the quality of the products and services provided to customers.

Visual Management and 6S

VISUAL MANAGEMENT IS a tool that is used to make processes and systems more visible to employees and customers. By making processes and systems more visible, businesses can identify areas for improvement and make changes to processes that will lead to better customer experiences.

The following are some of the most commonly used visual management tools:

Kanban: A visual signalling system that indicates when materials or parts are needed in a process. Kanban cards are used to trigger the replenishment of supplies.

Andon: A visual alert system used to signal a problem in a process, such as a breakdown or quality issue. Andon lights or displays are used to alert workers and managers to the problem.

Standardised work: Visual work instructions that provide a detailed description of how a task should be performed, including the sequence of steps, the tools and equipment needed, and the expected time for completion.

6S: A visual management system that involves Sorting, Simplifying, Sweeping, Standardizing, Sustaining, and making workspaces Safer. The goal is to create a clean, organized, safe and efficient workspace that reduces waste and improves productivity.

By using visual management tools, you can create a more efficient and productive workplace. Your team can quickly identify problems and take corrective action, reducing the risk of delays, errors, and customer complaints.

Visual management also helps you improve communication between different teams, leading to better collaboration and a stronger sense of ownership and accountability.

In retail and hospitality, visual management can be used to improve the customer experience by making processes more visible to customers. For example, if a customer is waiting for their food order at a restaurant, visual management can be used to show the customer the progress of their order and how much longer they will need to wait.

Chapter Summary/Key Takeaways

- Reducing queue times in a business is essential to providing an excellent customer experience.
- By identifying and eliminating waste in each of the eight areas, you can streamline your business processes and improve the efficiency and effectiveness of customer experience.
- By using Lean Manufacturing tools such as value stream mapping and waste reduction, you can streamline processes, reduce waiting times, and improve the overall experience for your customers.

Chapter 4: Applying Lean Tools to Reduce Waiting Times

―――

"If you don't rock the boat, folks, guess who's going to do it? Your competitors." - Todd Hockenberry, CEO of Top Line Results

LONG QUEUES AND WAIT times can have a significant negative impact on your customer experience. By using Lean Manufacturing tools such as the ones explained in Chapter 3, your business and team can identify and eliminate waste, reduce wait times and improve your customer experience.

Ultimately, reducing wait times and queues can lead to increased customer loyalty, improved brand perception, and increased profitability.

Lean Manufacturing has served us well as a systematic approach to identifying and eliminating waste in any process.

The purpose of this chapter is to show you some examples and templates that you can start using today, to reduce waiting times and queues that customers experience when interacting with your company's products or services.

Implementing Kaizen

KAIZEN OR CONTINUOUS Improvement can be implemented as simple as hearing ideas from your staff, then analysing and implementing as appropriate.

Here I'm showing an example of Kaizen using a restaurant service:

Step 1: Identify the Problem

The restaurant has noticed that customers are frequently experiencing or complaining about long wait times for their meals. In some cases, even abandoning the queues.

The leader in the restaurant brings a small team together to prepare and implement an improvement.

Step 2: Gather Information

The restaurant team collects data on wait times for each table and queues during a working week. They also identify the main bottlenecks in the kitchen and dining area.

Measure and establish metrics. Examples of metrics for this example could be: Reduce wait times by x%, improve customer satisfaction ratings by x%.

Step 3: Brainstorm Solutions

The team comes up with several potential solutions, such as reorganising the kitchen and drinks preparation layout, assigning more defined roles, improving communication between the kitchen and servers, and simplifying the menu to reduce preparation times.

Other strategies could involve: Preparing some ingredients in advance using forecast data to reduce cooking times, implementing a table reservation system to reduce waiting times, minimize unnecessary motion when staff move throughout the restaurant during the service process; place commonly used items in easily accessible locations to reduce movement.

Step 4: Test and Implement

The restaurant tests the potential solutions by implementing them in a small area or during off-peak hours. After analysing the results, the team decides to implement the changes permanently.

Step 5: Evaluate

The team evaluates the results by comparing current wait times to the previous ones. They also start gathering feedback from customers to ensure the changes have improved their experience.

When doing this kind of improvements, share the learnings such as: before and after metrics, and before and after pictures, so you can evaluate, learn and celebrate appropriately.

Lean Waste Audit Checklist

BY FREQUENTLY IDENTIFYING and eliminating waste, you can streamline your business processes and improve the efficiency and effectiveness of your customer experience. This is an example of a Lean Waste Audit that you can do in a regular basis.

This Lean audit can be done as frequently as necessary at the beginning of any improvement project. Depending on your situation you could do the audit at least 4 times per year.

An example of Lean Waste audit applied to a hospitality or restaurant business is shown here: as this is an example only, you can easily customise it for your process and business as required.

Overproduction

Are we preparing more food than needed?

Are we purchasing more supplies than required?

Are we scheduling more staff than necessary?

Are we overbooking reservations or events?

Waiting

Are customers waiting too long for service or food?

Are staff waiting for supplies, equipment, or orders?

Are there any bottlenecks in the process causing delays?

Are there any inefficient processes or procedures causing delays?

Overprocessing

Are we using more resources than needed?

Are we overpreparing food or drinks?

Are we performing unnecessary quality checks?

Are we duplicating work or processes?

Defects

Are we experiencing food waste due to overproduction?

Are we experiencing customer complaints due to poor quality food or service?

Are we experiencing delays due to errors?

Are we experiencing rework due to errors?

Excess Inventory

Are we ordering more supplies than required?

Are we storing excess inventory for long periods?

Are we using FIFO (first in, first out) to manage inventory?

Are we managing inventory levels effectively?

Unnecessary Motion

Are staff taking unnecessary steps or walking too much?

Are we optimizing workspace layouts?

Are we using ergonomic workstations?

Are we using technology to streamline processes?

Unused Talent

Are staff being utilized effectively?

Are staff members being cross-trained?

Are we utilizing the full potential of our workforce?

Are we providing training and development opportunities?

For more examples refer to the Appendix.

Value Stream mapping

VALUE STREAM MAPPING is a Lean Manufacturing tool that helps identify and eliminate waste in a process.

In the context of a restaurant, value stream mapping can be used to analyse the flow of orders, food preparation, and service delivery. By mapping the entire process, the restaurant can identify areas of waste, such as waiting times, unnecessary steps, and non-value-added activities.

Step 1: Identify the process to improve

In this case, the process to improve is the ordering process in the restaurant.

Step 2: Gather information

Collect data on the current ordering process, including the number of customers, average wait time, and customer feedback.

Step 3: Map the current state

Create a value stream map of the current ordering process, including all the steps involved and the time taken for each step. Identify any bottlenecks or delays in the process that contribute to long queuing times.

Step 4: Analyse the current state

Analyse the value stream map and identify areas for improvement. Determine which steps in the process can be eliminated, simplified, or combined to reduce wait times.

Step 5: Plan the future state

Using the information gathered in the previous steps, create a future state value stream map that shows the proposed changes to the ordering process. This should include new steps or process changes to reduce wait times.

Step 6: Implement the changes

Implement the changes identified in the future state value stream map. This may involve training staff, changing the layout of the restaurant, or implementing new technology.

Step 7: Monitor and review

Monitor the new process to ensure that it is working effectively and efficiently. Collect feedback from customers and staff to identify any further areas for improvement.

Keep in mind before and after metrics relevant to the improvement. As per this example, it could be the queuing times in minutes etc.

For more examples refer to the Appendix.

Spaghetti diagram

THIS IS BASED ON THE assumption of a case in a fast-food restaurant with a kitchen, dining area, and drive-thru:

1. Map out the kitchen area, including all workstations and equipment.
2. Observe the movement of employees and supplies in the kitchen during a typical service period.
3. Use a different coloured pen to track the path of each employee and supply (e.g., blue for the cook, red for the server, green for the ingredients).
4. Record the paths on the map to create a visual representation of the movement in the kitchen.
5. Analyse the diagram to identify areas of waste and inefficiency, such as employees having to walk back and forth frequently, or supplies being stored too far away from where they are needed.
6. Use the insights from the diagram to develop and implement improvement strategies, such as reorganising workstations or relocating supplies to reduce unnecessary motion.

For example, the diagram may show that the cook has to walk back and forth between the stove and the refrigerator several times during the preparation of a particular dish. By moving the refrigerator closer to the stove, the restaurant can eliminate unnecessary motion and improve efficiency.

Similarly, the diagram may show that the server has to travel a long distance to pick up a drink from the drink dispenser. By relocating the drink dispenser closer to the server station, the restaurant can improve customer service and reduce wait times.

For more examples refer to the Appendix.

Visual Management using a 6S Checklist

THIS CHECKLIST IS AN example that can be used to regularly review and evaluate the implementation of 6S principles in your business, helping to ensure a more efficient and effective operation that delivers a better customer experience.

Different to the Lean Waste Audit, the 6S Checklist is recommended to be done at least once per month and better on a weekly basis. Also, I have seen great results when the ownership is rotated between your staff to achieve collaboration and sustain the process.

This example is based on a hospitality business:

Sort

Are all unnecessary items removed from the workspace?

Are all tools and equipment properly stored and organised?

Are all materials and supplies properly labelled and stored?

Are all cleaning supplies properly stored and organised?

Set in order

Are all items in their designated locations?

Are all storage areas labelled and organised?

Are all tools and equipment stored in designated locations?

Are all materials and supplies properly labelled and stored?

Shine

Is the workspace clean and free of waste?

Are all tools and equipment properly cleaned and maintained?

Are all materials and supplies properly cleaned?

Standardise

Are all work instructions and procedures clearly defined and documented?

Are all tools and equipment properly calibrated and maintained?

Are all cleaning schedules and procedures clearly defined and documented?

Sustain

Are all employees consistently following 6S practices?

Are all employees trained on 6S principles and practices?

Are all work areas and equipment being regularly maintained and cleaned?

Safety

Are all safety hazards identified and addressed promptly?

Are all employees trained on safety procedures?

Are all safety procedures clearly documented and communicated to all employees?

For more examples that you can adapt, refer to the Appendix.

Chapter Summary/Key Takeaways

- Starting to use the lean waste or 6S checklist can help you identify quick wins to make your business more efficient and improve your customer experience.
- Using the examples provided, you can adapt to your business and start identifying and eliminating waste in any process.
- Start testing and using the templates provided, you can easily build up from there.
- Start with small improvements every day and you will build the continuous improvement culture in your business and team.

PART III: Expanding Your Service Culture

EXPANDING YOUR SERVICE Culture is dedicated to exploring ways in which your business can build a customer-centric culture that extends beyond the basics of customer service.

This section will provide insights into how businesses can create a holistic approach to customer service, where the customer experience is woven into every aspect of the organization, from leadership to employee training and development.

By adopting a service culture, businesses can differentiate themselves from competitors, increase customer loyalty, and drive growth.

The chapters in this section will explore into strategies for embedding a customer-centric culture into your business, such as leadership practices, employee engagement and technology use.

EDUARDO J. ESTRADA

Chapter 5: Creating a Culture of Continuous Improvement

"An extraordinary life is all about daily, continuous improvements in the areas that matter most."- Robin Sharma

CONTINUOUS IMPROVEMENT is the process of continuously refining all aspects of an organization, from its products and services to its processes, policies, and procedures.

Creating a culture of continuous improvement is crucial for any organization that wants to stay competitive in today's fast-paced business environment.

In this chapter, we will discuss how to create a culture of continuous improvement focused on customer experience improvements. We will also explore some of the tools that can be used to achieve this goal, and two case studies of organizations that have successfully created a culture of continuous improvement in customer service.

Creating a Culture of Continuous Improvement

CREATING A CULTURE of continuous improvement is not an easy task, but it is essential to ensure the success of any organization. The first step in creating a culture of continuous improvement is to establish a clear vision and mission for the organization.

This vision, mission and strategies should be communicated to all employees, so they understand the organization's purpose and goals. Once this is done, the organization needs to create a culture of constant learning, support and growth.

This can be achieved through training, coaching, and mentoring programs that empower employees to develop their skills and knowledge.

Another important aspect of creating a culture of continuous improvement is to foster an environment of innovation and creativity. This can be achieved by encouraging employees to come up with new ideas and solutions to problems, where all are quickly taken into account and implemented or put on hold until a better moment.

The organization should also provide the necessary resources and support to turn these ideas into action. Moreover, it's essential to recognise and reward employees' contributions to the organization's success, which will motivate them to continuously improve.

Examples of Organizations with a Culture of Continuous Improvement in Customer Experience

TOYOTA IS A LEADING automotive manufacturer that has successfully created a culture of continuous improvement. The company's philosophy is based on the concept of Kaizen, which is normally considered a synonym of continuous improvement.

Toyota encourages all employees to identify and eliminate waste, improve processes, and enhance customer satisfaction. The company has a strong focus on customer service, and its employees are trained to provide excellent service to customers.

According to an article about Toyota culture (Sturdevant, 2014) "applying Lean is a leadership challenge, not just an operational one. A company's senior executives often become successful as leaders through years spent learning how to contribute inside a particular culture. Indeed, Toyota views this as a career-long process and encourages it by offering executives a diversity of assignments, significant amounts of training".

Toyota's continuous improvement efforts have resulted in several benefits, including increased efficiency, reduced costs, and improved customer satisfaction. In the J.D. Power Customer Service Index (JD Power, 2023), which measures customer satisfaction with dealer services, Toyota or associated brands normally rank on the top places.

Another arguable example of a company that is customer focused is Amazon, with the launch of Amazon Go, which is a relevant example for this book.

Amazon Go is a new kind of store with no checkout required. Amazon Go claims to have "created the world's most advanced retail technology so you never have to wait in line." (Amazon, n.d.) Users can simply walk into the store, check-in with their app and then start taking items from the shelves as they go, without needing to stand in line at the checkout counter at the end. Ultimately, they are charged through the app and their Amazon account.

At the beginning of the implementation of Amazon Go stores, the company faced challenges in delivering a seamless customer experience.

Amazon leveraged its culture of continuous improvement to address the challenges facing its stores. The company formed a cross-functional team composed of engineers, data analysts, and customer service representatives. The team's primary goal was to identify and eliminate the root causes of the accuracy issues. The team began by using lean tools, including value stream mapping and root cause analysis, to understand the underlying issues. They then developed a continuous improvement plan that included upgrading the computer vision technology, refining the machine learning algorithms, and improving the training of the system. The team also implemented new customer service protocols, such as offering refunds and free items to customers who experienced issues with the system. This approach helped to build trust with customers and demonstrate the company's commitment to continuous improvement.

Amazon Go's culture of continuous improvement led to significant improvements in the accuracy of the system. Customers reported fewer issues with incorrect charges and misidentified items, leading to increased satisfaction and repeat business.

The company was also able to improve the efficiency of its stores, resulting in reduced wait times and increased customer throughput.

Coaching to improve your business culture

STAFF TRAINING IS ESSENTIAL for providing excellent customer experience. The team should be trained to understand and meet customer expectations, handle customer complaints effectively, and provide consistent service across all locations.

Coaching and training are essential elements in creating a culture of continuous improvement in customer experience. At the end training helps staff to develop the skills and knowledge necessary to provide exceptional service to customers.

Coaching is a process that involves providing feedback and guidance to employees to help them improve their skills and performance; it is an essential tool for improving customer experience because it helps employees understand their strengths and weaknesses and how they can improve their performance. It also helps employees to develop the necessary skills to provide exceptional service to customers. This should be an ongoing process that takes place regularly. Managers and supervisors should provide regular feedback to employees, highlighting areas where they excel and areas where they need improvement. This feedback should be specific, constructive, and actionable, providing employees with the necessary information and support to improve their performance.

In addition to providing feedback, coaching should also involve setting goals and objectives. This will help employees to focus on their development and track their progress. Managers and supervisors should work with employees to set achievable goals that are aligned with the organization's objectives. Goals should be specific, measurable, achievable, relevant, and time-bound.

In the Lean philosophy there is a term called Coaching Kata. The term "Kata" comes from martial arts and means "a series of recorded movements". The idea of the coaching Kata is to have a few predefined steps that must be completed from the current situation to a target state.

Coaching Kata is normally executed by asking the following 5 questions:

- What is your goal or target state?
- What is your current state?
- What obstacles are preventing you from reaching the goal state?
- What is your next step?
- When can we go and see what we have learned from taking this step?

Training

TRAINING IS ANOTHER essential tool for improving customer experience. It provides employees with the knowledge and skills necessary to provide exceptional service to customers. Training can be provided in various forms, including classroom training, online training, and on-the-job training.

Effective training programs should be tailored to the specific needs of your staff and your organization. The training should be designed to help employees understand your organization's products and services, customer needs and expectations, and how to provide exceptional service.

Any training can take time to prepare but it should provide employees with the necessary skills to handle customer complaints and resolve problems.

Although new employees normally receive comprehensive training to help them understand the organization's culture, values, and expectations, training programs should also be ongoing to ensure that employees are continually developing their skills and knowledge.

Existing employees should also receive regular training to keep them up to date with new products, services, and technologies.

Coaching and training are essential tools for creating a culture of continuous improvement in customer experience. They help employees develop the skills and knowledge necessary to provide exceptional service to customers.

Chapter Summary/Key Takeaways

- Creating a culture of continuous improvement is crucial for any organization that wants to stay competitive in today's business environment.
- Focusing on customer experience improvements is essential to achieve success in a sustainable manner.
- Using the power of a culture of continuous improvement and waste elimination in your processes, you can deliver a seamless customer experience.
- Engaging and investing in your staff can help build trust with customers and maintain your position as a leader in your sector.
- Using Coaching and the coaching Kata questions can help your team to go from a current situation to an ideal situation or target state.

Chapter 6: Leveraging Technology to Enhance Customer Experience

"If you need a new process and don't install it, you pay for it without getting it." - Ken Stork, Motorola

TECHNOLOGY CAN BE USED to improve customer experience, such as using mobile apps, online ordering, and self-checkout kiosks. However, it's essential that you ensure that technology is integrated seamlessly into your customer experience and does not worsen it.

As the cost of opportunity demonstrates, sometimes the option to adopting necessary technology to improve customer experience can result in a significant return on investment rather than spending for all the maintenance of your old process. Essentially, you could spend the same amount (or more) fixing your outdated systems as you would investing in a new process or system that could significantly improve your client experience.

With Artificial intelligence (AI) taking the world and rapidly advancing the way businesses operate, AI can be used in many ways to improve customer service in any business, such as personalising your customer experience, optimising operations, and reducing wait times.

In this chapter, we will discuss how technology can be leveraged to enhance customer service in businesses.

Personalization

PERSONALIZATION IS a key component of excellent customer service. Customers appreciate when their needs and preferences are understood and catered to.

While your company is still small, personalization is easily achieved, however when your operation starts growing the data from your customers becomes really difficult to handle, potentially making your client's experience less personal.

Personalization is an essential part of providing customers with a unique and tailored experience. Technology can surely help your businesses achieve this. Here are suggestions that you can take to implement technology applications and enhance customer experience through personalization:

1. **Using your customer data:** The first step is to gather information about your customers, such as their preferences, purchase history, and behaviour patterns. Always following the latest privacy policies and your customer consent, this data can be collected through surveys, social media, or loyalty programs.
2. **Analyse customer data:** Once you have collected customer data, the next step is to analyse it to identify patterns and trends. This analysis can help you understand customer behaviour, preferences, and needs.
3. **Develop customer personas:** Based on the data analysis, businesses can create customer personas that represent your ideal customers. These personas can help tailor your products and services to meet your customers' needs better. Although, this is still a generalisation, it can help you narrow down your offers. This information can then be used to create personalized recommendations and promotions.
4. **Use personalization tools:** There are many technology tools available that can help your businesses personalize the customer experience, such as recommendation engines, chatbots, and targeted marketing campaigns. Identify the areas where virtual assistants or chatbots can provide the most value to customers, such as order taking, customer support, or

recommendations.

5. **Implement tools such as chatbot or other Artificial Intelligence:** AI technology can be used to personalize customer experiences by analysing data in real-time to provide relevant and personalized recommendations to customers. Choose the right platform and tools to develop chatbots. Some popular platforms include Dialogflow, IBM Watson Assistant, and Amazon Lex.

6. **Monitor and evaluate:** Finally, it is essential to monitor and evaluate the impact of any technology applications on your customer experience. This analysis can help you identify areas for improvement so you can adjust any personalization strategies.

Leveraging technology to enhance customer experience through personalization can help businesses stand out from your competitors and build strong relationships with customers.

By following these steps, you can create a more personalized experience that meets the unique needs of your customers.

Optimising Operations

THE USE OF TECHNOLOGY can greatly enhance the efficiency of operations in your business. By implementing the right technologies, you can reduce costs, improve service, and increase customer satisfaction.

Here are some standard steps to implement technology in your daily operations:

1. **Identify the areas for improvement:** The first step is to identify the areas of operations that can be improved by technology. You can use some of the lean tools mentioned before. This may include inventory management, order

processing, customer service, and payment processing.

2. **Research and select appropriate technologies:** Once you have identified the areas for improvement, research and select appropriate technologies that can help you optimize your operations. This may include point-of-sale systems, inventory management software, and customer relationship management (CRM) tools.

3. **Implement and integrate the technologies:** Once you have selected the appropriate technologies, it's time to implement and integrate them into your operations. This may involve training staff on how to use the new systems and integrating them with existing software and hardware.

4. **Monitor and measure the impact:** After the implementation, it's important to monitor and measure the impact of the new technologies on your operations. This can help you identify areas that need further improvement and adjust your strategies accordingly.

Although you may be using your favourite tools for optimising operations, here showing some examples of tools that can improve efficiency and reduce costs in your businesses:

Point-of-sale system (POS): These allow businesses to accept payments and manage inventory on-the-go. It also provides analytics and reporting tools to help you track sales and understand customer behaviour.

Project management tools: help businesses manage tasks, projects, and workflows. It provides a visual management interface for organizing tasks and assigning responsibilities, which can help teams work more efficiently.

Customer Relationship Management (CRM): allow businesses engage with customers and collect customer data. It provides a platform for sending targeted marketing campaigns, tracking customer behaviour, and analysing customer feedback.

By leveraging technology and implementing the right applications, you can optimize your operations, improve your bottom line and reduce wait times while providing excellent customer service.

Optimising the Queue

LONG WAIT TIMES CAN lead to frustration and lost business. Lean management and technology can assist you in managing and even reducing wait times during peak hours.

What optimisation would you make if you were attempting to reduce the time spent in your business' queues? There are several queuing optimisation techniques that can be used in any company, from retail, hospitality, healthcare to any type of small business.

Some ideas that incorporate the use of Lean tools and technology include:

Self-Checkout Systems or Queue Management Systems: These systems are a mix of software and hardware that provides your company with the tools it needs to watch, plan, forecast, and control the customer's experience from arrival to exit. By using this system, you can improve the flow of customers through a physical store, reduce wait times, and provide real-time information on wait times and available service points. These systems can use the First-In-First-Out (FIFO) principle or of first-come-first-served, which minimizes wait times for customers.

Mobile Queuing: Mobile queuing systems allow customers to join a virtual queue and receive notifications on their mobile devices when it is their turn to be served, reducing the need to wait in a physical queue.

Multi-Channel Queuing: Multi-channel queuing involves offering multiple service points, such as self-checkout, mobile, and traditional checkout counters, to help manage customer demand and reduce wait times. With the use of AI technology, it can become easier for forecasting and delivering a great customer experience.

Appointment Scheduling: Appointments can be scheduled to reduce the number of customers in the store at any given time, and to provide a more personalized shopping experience.

Line Busting: Line busting involves using mobile devices, such as tablets, to process transactions and assist customers, reducing the need for them to wait in line. It is especially important in retail settings, where long lines can wrap through the store, cause overcrowding, and deter customers from entering the store or making a purchase. You may have already used this during the pandemic, as it can also be called "click and collect" or "buy online, pick-up in store", where the customer pre-pays for an item, usually online, and picks it up at the store.

Increase staffing levels during peak hours: Using specific planning apps and based in your customer data, you can easily forecast when you should have additional staff available during busy periods. This can help you reduce the wait time for customers.

Train staff to work more efficiently: Ensure that your staff are trained and equipped to handle customers quickly and efficiently, this can help to reduce wait times. Nowadays with the use of videos, digital work instructions, and even augmented reality, it is easier to train staff more efficiently on the task at hand.

Optimize the layout of the store: Following the Lean tools presented before, you can use simple drawing programs, to ensure the layout of your store, business or shop allows for an efficient flow of customers and materials, and that the queue lines are well organized.

SORRY ABOUT THE WAIT

Implementing these optimizations will require careful planning and ongoing monitoring, but they can help to significantly reduce wait times and improve the customer experience in your business or store.

It's important to evaluate the specific needs of your business, and to choose the queuing optimizations that are most appropriate and effective for your customers.

Regularly monitor and measure wait times and make ongoing improvements to your queuing strategy to ensure that wait times are minimized and the customer experience is improved.

Chapter Summary/Key Takeaways

- Artificial intelligence is a powerful tool that can be used to improve customer service in any business.
- By personalizing the customer experience, optimizing operations, and reducing wait times, businesses can provide an excellent customer experience and gain a competitive edge.
- As AI and other technologies continues to evolve, it will become increasingly important for businesses to leverage it to enhance their customer service.
- It's important to evaluate the specific needs of your business and start small, testing your queuing optimizations that are most appropriate and effective for your customers.
- Don't forget to monitor and measure the impact of the new technologies on your operations.

Conclusion

IN CONCLUSION, THIS book aimed to provide a comprehensive guide to improving customer experience in any small business, including hospitality, healthcare and retail industries, through the lens of lean management and technology.

We began by exploring the fundamentals of customer experience and Lean Manufacturing, which laid the foundation for the tools and techniques we discussed in the subsequent chapters.

Through the application of lean tools such as Kaizen, value stream mapping, spaghetti diagrams, and 6S, we demonstrated how businesses can streamline their operations, reduce waiting times, and ultimately enhance the customer experience. We also highlighted the importance of a culture of continuous improvement, where everyone in the organization is encouraged to contribute to the improvement of processes and systems.

Finally, we discussed the role of technology in improving customer experience, particularly through personalization and the use of virtual assistants and chatbots. We presented several examples of technology applications that businesses can use to optimize operations, reduce costs, and improve efficiency.

As we conclude, the lessons learned from this book are that improving customer experience requires a combination of understanding customer needs, optimizing operations through Lean tools and techniques, creating a culture of continuous improvement, and leveraging technology to enhance personalization and efficiency. By implementing these strategies, businesses can deliver exceptional customer experiences, increase customer loyalty, and ultimately achieve long-term success.

References

(2023). Retrieved from JD Power: https://www.jdpower.com/business/automotive/us-customer-service-index-csi-study

Amazon. (n.d.). *Amazon.Go.* Retrieved from https://us.amazon.com/gp/help/customer/display.html?nodeId=GWDXYUM9SFHE35KD

Chambers, S. (n.d.). *The Art of Saying Sorry – How to Apologize in Customer Service.* Retrieved from https://www.nicereply.com/blog/customer-service-apology/

Lassen, M. (n.d.). *10 Better Ways to Say "Sorry to Keep You Waiting"*. Retrieved from https://grammarhow.com/better-ways-to-say-sorry-to-keep-you-waiting-email/

PhD, N. M. (2021). *What's Happened to Our Attention Spans During the Pandemic?* Retrieved from psychologytoday.com: https://www.psychologytoday.com/us/blog/communications -matter/202103/whats-happened-our-attention-spans-during-the-pandemic

PwC. (2018). *Experience is everything: here's how to get it right.* PwC. Retrieved from https://www.pwc.com/us/en/advisory-services/publications/consumer-intelligence-series/pwc-consumer-intelligence-series-customer-experience.pdf

Sturdevant, D. (2014). *(Still) learning from Toyota.* Retrieved from McKinsey Quarterly: https://www.mckinsey.com/

industries/automotive-and-assembly/our-insights/still-learning-from-toyota

Waitwhile. (2022). *The State of Waiting in Line*. Waitwhile survey. Retrieved 2023, from https://waitwhile.com/blog/consumer-survey-waiting-in-line/

ZenDesk. (2022). *CX Trends 2022*. ZenDesk. Retrieved 2023, from https://www.zendesk.com/au/sg/customer-experience-trends/#report

SORRY ABOUT THE WAIT

Acknowledgments

———

WRITING A BOOK IS A challenging effort, and this project would not have been possible without the support and assistance of many people. I would like to express my sincere gratitude to the following people:

First and foremost, a heartfelt thank you to all my family for their genuine support throughout this project. Their patience, encouragement, and understanding were invaluable in making this book a reality.

I would like to express my sincere gratitude to Rocio Ampie for creating such a beautiful cover for my book. Your creativity and attention to detail have made this book stand out and I am truly grateful for your hard work and dedication

I would also like to thank my colleagues and mentors along the years, who provided me guidance and expertise throughout my professional development to be able to write this book. Their insights and perspectives were instrumental in shaping its contents.

Special thanks to the editors and publishing team who worked tirelessly to bring this book to fruition. Their professionalism and attention to detail ensured the final product was of the highest quality.

Finally, I would like to express gratitude to the readers of this book, to you who have taken the time to engage with these ideas and concepts presented here. It is your curiosity and dedication that inspires me to continue exploring the world of Lean Manufacturing and business process improvement.

Thank you all for your contributions and support. This book would not have been possible without your help.

Appendix

Example of Lean Waste Audit Checklist for a Manufacturing Company

FOR EACH OF THE QUESTIONS write your Observation and a recommended Improvement if needed:

- Are we producing more than what is demanded?
- Are we storing more inventory than required?
- Are we producing too much too soon?
- Are workers waiting for parts, instructions, or equipment?
- Are machines waiting for materials, maintenance, or repairs?
- Are workers idle because of the lack of work?
- Are there any bottlenecks in the process that are causing delays?
- Are we doing more work than required?
- Are we using more resources than necessary?
- Are we performing unnecessary quality checks?
- Are we producing defective products?
- Are we experiencing rework?
- Are we having to scrap materials?
- Are we storing excess inventory for long periods?
- Are we ordering more than what is required?
- Are we using FIFO (first in, first out) to manage inventory?
- Are workers taking unnecessary steps or walking too much?
- Are we using ergonomic workstations?
- Are we optimizing workspace layouts?
- Are we using gravity-fed conveyors?
- Are we using workers effectively?
- Are workers being cross-trained?
- Are we utilizing the full potential of our workforce?
- Are we providing training and development opportunities?

•

Example of Lean Waste Audit Checklist for a Healthcare Facility:

FOR EACH OF THE QUESTIONS write your Observation and a recommended Improvement if needed:

Overproduction

Are we ordering more medical supplies than required?

Are we scheduling more appointments than required?

Are we having patients wait unnecessarily?

Waiting

Are patients waiting for too long to be seen?

Are patients waiting for test results?

Are there any bottlenecks in the process that are causing delays?

Overprocessing

Are we performing unnecessary tests or procedures?

Are we using excessive resources?

Are we using multiple forms or systems to manage patient information?

Defects

Are we experiencing delays due to errors?

Are we having to cancel or reschedule appointments due to errors?

Excess Inventory

Are we ordering more medical supplies than required?

Are we overstocking medication or medical supplies?

Are we using a FIFO (first in, first out) system to manage inventory?

Unnecessary Motion

Are staff members walking too much or taking unnecessary steps?

Are we optimizing workspace layouts?

Are we using technology to streamline processes?

Unused Talent

Are staff members being utilized effectively? providing training and development opportunities?

Are staff members being cross-trained?

Example of Value Stream Map to reduce queuing times in a Healthcare environment:

STEP 1: DEFINE THE problem and scope

The problem is long waiting times for patients in the emergency department of a hospital. The scope includes the entire patient flow from check-in to discharge.

Step 2: Map the current state

Create a visual map of the current patient flow, including all processes and the time taken for each. This should identify where bottlenecks are occurring and where queues are forming.

Step 3: Identify waste and opportunities for improvement

Analyse the current state map to identify any waste in the process. This could include overproduction, waiting, unnecessary movement, over-processing, excess inventory, defects, and unused talent. Identify areas where improvements can be made, such as reducing wait times at triage, improving communication between departments, and streamlining the discharge process.

Step 4: Map the future state

Create a visual map of the improved patient flow, incorporating the changes identified in the previous step. This should include new processes and the estimated time taken for each.

Step 5: Implement

Implement the changes and measure to ensure they are effective. This could involve measuring waiting times, patient satisfaction levels, and the number of patients treated per hour.

Step 6: Monitor and review

Ensure that the improvements are sustained over time and continue to monitor the process to identify further opportunities for improvement. This could involve regularly reviewing patient flow, collecting feedback from patients and staff, and making any necessary adjustments.

Examples of metrics could be waiting times in minutes, patient satisfaction levels.

Example of creating a spaghetti diagram for a hospital:

1. **Select the area to be studied:** Identify the area of the hospital where patients frequently wait in queues or experience delays. This could be the emergency department, outpatient clinic, or radiology department.
2. **Collect data:** Observe and record the movements of patients and staff in the selected area for a set period of time. Note the location, duration, and frequency of each movement.
3. **Create a floor plan:** Draw a floor plan of the selected area, including all relevant features such as doors, furniture, and equipment.
4. **Plot the lines:** Using the floor plan, plot the movements of patients and staff as lines or paths. Use different colours to differentiate between patients and staff, and between different types of movements (e.g., walking, sitting, waiting).
5. **Analyse the diagram:** Review the diagram to identify areas where patients and staff are experiencing unnecessary or excessive movements. Look for areas where bottlenecks or congestion occur, and where improvements can be made.
6. **Implement improvements:** Once you have identified areas for improvement, work with staff and stakeholders to implement changes that will reduce unnecessary movements and improve patient flow. Examples of improvements could include rearranging furniture, adjusting staffing levels, or redesigning the layout of the area.
7. **Monitor and evaluate:** Monitor the area after changes have been implemented to evaluate the effectiveness of the improvements. Use data to measure the impact of the changes on patient flow, waiting times, and staff satisfaction.

BY FOLLOWING THESE steps, you can create a spaghetti diagram to identify areas of waste and opportunities for improvement in a hospital setting.

Example of a 6S checklist for a Gym business:

FOR EACH OF THE QUESTIONS write your Observation and a recommended Improvement if needed:

Sort

Are all gym equipment, supplies, and materials necessary for daily use available?

Are unused equipment, supplies, and materials removed from the gym area?

Are items stored in the correct location?

Set in order

Are all gym equipment, supplies, and materials arranged in a neat and organized manner?

Are gym equipment and supplies labelled for easy identification?

Are storage areas and shelves clean and tidy?

Shine

Are gym floors, walls, mirrors, and windows clean and free from smudges and stains?

Are gym equipment and machines wiped down and sanitized regularly?

Are locker rooms and restrooms kept clean and well-stocked?

Standardise

Are there standard operating procedures in place for gym staff to follow?

Are all gym equipment, supplies, and materials consistently arranged and labeled?

Are cleaning and maintenance schedules established and adhered to?

Sustain

Is there a system in place to maintain the 6S standards?

Are employees trained on the importance of maintaining 6S standards?

Are regular audits performed to ensure that 6S standards are being upheld?

Safety

Are safety hazards identified and addressed promptly?

Are gym equipment and machines inspected regularly for safety issues?

Are safety rules and procedures clearly posted and communicated to employees and gym members?

Don't miss out!

Visit the website below and you can sign up to receive emails whenever Eduardo J. Estrada publishes a new book. There's no charge and no obligation.

https://books2read.com/r/B-A-HFWX-HDUHC

BOOKS 2 READ

Connecting independent readers to independent writers.

About the Author

Eduardo J. Estrada is an experienced Industrial Engineer with a professional background in Sustainability, Quality and Lean management. With over 15 years of experience, the author has worked extensively in the manufacturing industry, identifying, and implementing process improvements to enhance efficiency and reduce waste.

The author has been recognized for his contributions to sustainability and operations excellence, having been instrumental in winning awards for the companies where he has worked. Currently residing in Australia with his family, the author enjoys spending his free time travelling, cycling, reading, and working on improving business processes.

With a passion for continuous improvement and a deep understanding of Lean Manufacturing tools, the author brings a wealth of knowledge and expertise to this book. Through his work, the author aims to help organizations reduce wait times and queues, improve customer experience, and drive business success.

If you want to learn more about these topics or would like to start a conversation, you can reach out at: theleanmate@outlook.com